July 1980

To Matthew
With love from Grandma

The Red Ochre People

The Red Ochre People

How Newfoundland's Beothuck Indians Lived

Ingeborg Marshall

Illustrations by Martin Springett

J.J. Douglas Ltd.
Vancouver

For Bill, Alfred, Christopher, Mary-Anne

J.J. Douglas Ltd.
1875 Welch Street
North Vancouver
Canada V7P 1B7

Canadian Cataloguing in Publication Data

Marshall, Ingeborg, 1929-
   The red ochre people

   Includes index.
   ISBN 0-88894-157-9

   1. Beothuk Indians.   I. Title.
   E99.B4M37   971.8'004'97   C77-002145-X

Typesetting by Domino-Link Word and Data Processing Ltd.
Design realized by Nicholas Newbeck
Jacket art by Karen Harris
Printed and bound in Canada by the Hunter Rose Company, Toronto

Contents

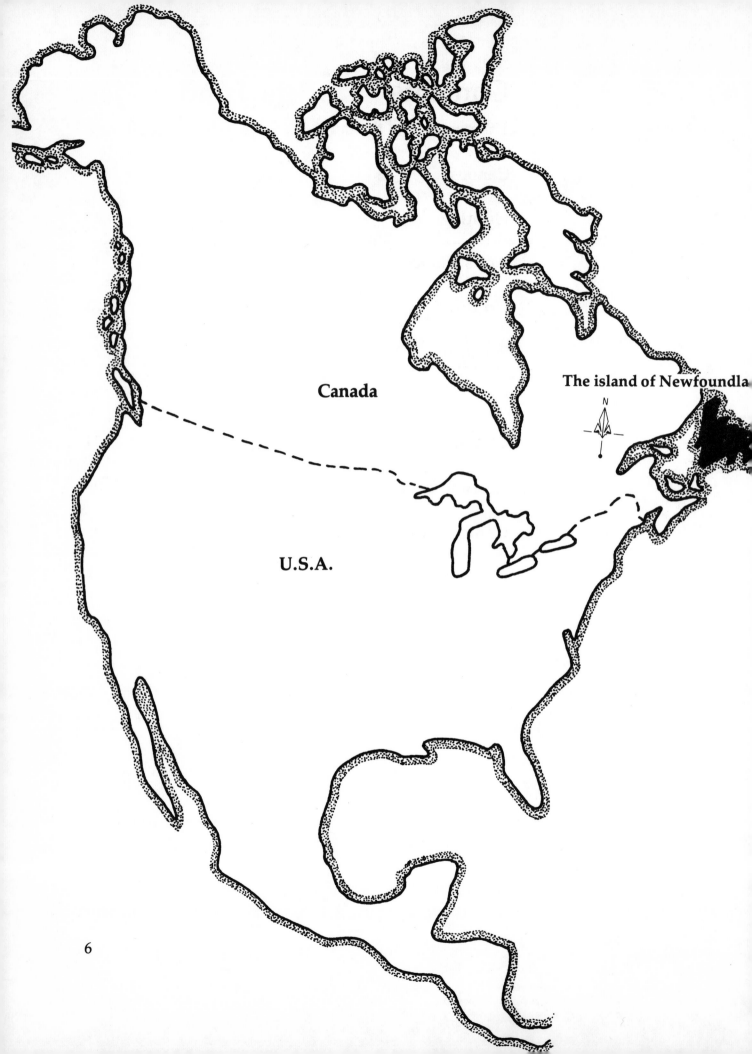

Canada

The island of Newfoundla

U.S.A.

The People and the Land

The Beothucks lived on the island of Newfoundland for many centuries until the last of them died nearly 150 years ago. Stories about them are still told by the older people in the outport fishing communities, and once in a while some of their remains are found by fishermen or archeologists. They were tall, strong people with dark eyes and long, black hair, part of which they braided at the back of the head and decorated with feathers. The Beothucks dressed in animal skins, hunted with bows and arrows, and covered their bodies, clothes and weapons with a mixture of red ochre and oil. This mixture protected against the cold in winter and the insects in summer; the ochre was also believed to have a life-giving power. White people called the Beothucks "Red Indians" because of their ochre-covered skin, which to Europeans looked frightening.

Beothuck remains found

The Beothuck Indians were not the first people to discover and live on the island of Newfoundland. Thousands of years earlier, an ancient race of Indians which we call the Maritime Archaic Indians had occupied these coasts for a time. Occasionally some of their elaborate burial places and large polished stone tools are found near the shores. Possibly the Beothuck Indians were related to these early Maritime people. We do not know exactly when the Beothucks first came to the island. For a while they may have moved back and forth from the coast of Labrador to Newfoundland across the Strait of Belle Isle, which is at one point only 12 miles wide. By about 200 AD the Beothuck Indians were probably well settled in Newfoundland, and later they no longer moved off the island. Here they developed their own culture, though they were still part of the Algonquin family of tribes.

Another group of native people to have lived on the coasts of Newfoundland were the Dorset Eskimos. They came from the Cape Dorset regions far in the north around 500 BC and stayed on the Newfoundland shores for about one thousand years. It is likely that they met with the Beothuck Indians, and on occasion they may have exchanged some of their tools or fought in battle against each other. Eventually the Dorset Eskimos died out, leaving the island to the Beothuck Indians.

The island of Newfoundland was a rich hunting and fishing ground that was well suited to support hunting people. Large herds of caribou grazed on lichen in "the barrens." Bear, beaver, wolf, lynx and smaller mammals lived in the pine and fir forests which stretched from coast to coast. Thousands of inland ponds and waterways teemed with trout and salmon. The surrounding sea provided fish and other foods. In spring, seals and whales came to the shores, and seabirds were plentiful. The island's subarctic summers are warm but short and the winters long-lasting, cold and stormy with much snow. The Indians knew how to equip themselves well for such weather.

Canoes

We are not sure how the Beothuck Indians reached Newfoundland. They could have walked over the Strait of Belle Isle when the water froze in mid-winter, or they may have paddled across in their canoes in summer from the coasts of Labrador in the north or Nova Scotia in the southwest. Although canoeing in the sea is dangerous, the Beothuck canoes were very seaworthy, differing in their design from all other Indian canoes. We know what they looked like because early settlers and explorers wrote about them in their diaries and letters, and canoes were found in abandoned Beothuck camps, although unfortunately no one preserved a canoe for a museum. All we have left now are some canoe models made of birch bark covered with red ochre that were found in Beothuck burial graves, and they give only the shape of the canoe without details of its construction. They were made of a framework of spruce and then covered with birch bark.

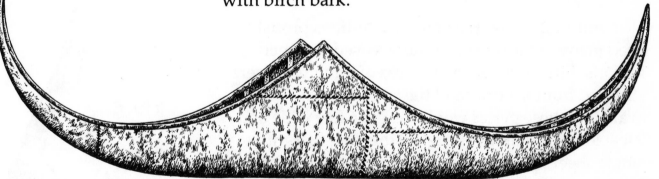

Birch bark canoe

Unlike most canoes, they curved high at both ends, and the sides rose in the middle as shown in the drawing. Instead of having a flat or rounded bottom like other bark canoes, the Beothuck ones had fairly straight sides and a keel so that the canoe could cut through waves better. The keel also prevented the canoe from being blown off course. The upward curve at the stem and stern made it able to go forward or backward with equal swiftness, and the peaked sides kept waves from swamping the boat in rough water.

Seaworthy canoes were essential, because the Indians often traveled on the ocean. Their burial places have been found on islands many miles out to sea; they even went as far as the Funk Islands to hunt birds and collect eggs of the now extinct great auk. The Funk Islands are 35 miles out into the North Atlantic, and to travel that far is a daring voyage for a canoe propelled only by paddles.

Great auk

Canoe paddle

In building canoes the Beothuck Indians probably used many of the same techniques used by other Indians. First, several good pieces of birch bark were stripped from the trunks of the largest trees available; these pieces would be 4 to 6 feet wide and 3 feet long, and they were sewn together to form a single sheet large enough to cover most of the canoe. Next, long pieces of spruce were tapered and shaped into a frame for the keel and the curved stem and stern. These were lashed together with split roots. Then the bark sheet was laid out on the ground and the keel, stem and stern structure, all in one piece, was placed on top, in the center. With the help of stakes driven into the ground, the bark was folded up to form the sides. Now the upper edges of the

uilding a birch bark canoe

sides (gunwales) were put into place and tied to the stem and stern poles. The edges of the birch bark sheet were folded over the gunwales and lashed securely onto them.

At both the curved ends, the bark had to be cut and sewn together under the keel. Once this stitching was completed, the two sides of the canoe were sprung apart wide enough so that cross bars or "thwarts" could be placed at the middle and at each end to hold the sides in position. Finally the sides were strengthened with flattened sticks laid lengthwise to cover the birch bark inside. Shorter sticks were inserted like ribs from the keel to the edge, securing them to the gunwale. A second or "false" gunwale was fitted around the outside edge of the boat to serve as a fender. All sewing was done with split roots, and looked like neat basketwork. The seams were waterproofed with a thick coating of tree gum and red ochre.

11

Because Beothuck canoes were very light and had a keel, they would not stay upright in the water without stones laid in the bottom. The Indians covered this rock ballast with moss and sod so that it was more comfortable to kneel upon when they were paddling. A canoe could be from 14 to 22 feet long, and it could hold from four to eight adults.

No one, it seems, has made a full-sized copy of a Beothuck canoe and tried it for seaworthiness. This would be an interesting project to do—to see how it floats and how much ballast of rocks is required to keep it upright in the water.

Canoes were the most important means of transportation inland as well as at sea. The Beothucks had no horses or dogs to help them carry their loads, and it was difficult to penetrate the heavy undergrowth of the forests on foot, or to avoid the many inland marshes. The easiest and quickest way of traveling was by canoe along the chains of ponds and rivers, portaging the light bark vessels around rapids or across land barriers. It has been said that a strong man could lift a canoe with one hand onto his shoulder.

In winter, of course, the inland waterways were frozen, and as soon as there was enough snow on the ground the Indians used sledges to transport their belongings from one place to another. For walking over snow and ice, they used snowshoes. The frame of a snowshoe was made by bending a length of supple wood into a loop and then lashing the two ends together to form a trailing tail at the back. Then two crossbars were laced to the frame, and the open spaces were skillfully webbed with wet seal or caribou-hide strips. As the skin strips dried out, they became tight. A snowshoe was 3½ feet long including the one-foot-long tail which counterbalanced the weight of the front so that the shoe would not tip forward. The ends were raised slightly to prevent snow from collecting on the shoe's surface.

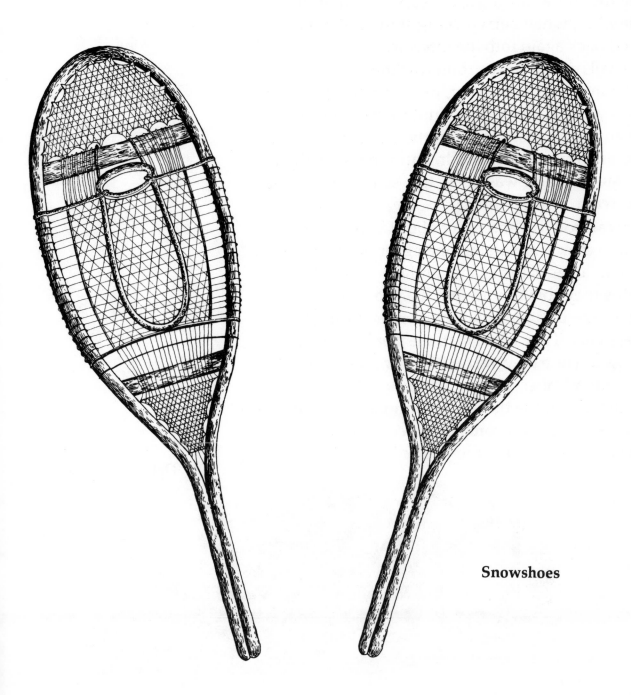

Snowshoes

Hunting

The Beothuck Indians were migratory people, moving with the seasons from the inland areas to the seashores and back again. In fall they hunted caribou inland; in spring they went to the coasts to catch seals. Birds' eggs and seafood were gathered along the shores during spring and summer. In September, when berrypicking started, the Indians moved back again into the interior.

The fall hunt of the caribou was the most important event in the year, marking the approach of heavy snows that would limit food gathering for the winter months. Large numbers of caribou were killed and the meat stored. In autumn the caribou were fat. Their fur was thick, too, so that their hides made warm winter clothes.

The caribou live and move about in herds. In summer they graze on the open ground in the northern areas of the island, and for the winter months they come south into the shelter of the forests. The best time to hunt them is during their travel in fall. They take much the same route every year, and while they are on the move they always follow their leader. Knowing this enabled the Beothucks to guide the leading animals into a trap so that enough caribou could be killed to provide for many families through the winter.

Detail of deer fence

Tasseled poles for directing caribou

In early fall the families would meet at a river where they expected the caribou herds to cross. They would build fences along both sides of the river, leaving only a few openings for the animals to come through. They made fences by felling trees which grew along the river banks. The trees were left hanging onto the stumps so that the trunks formed a kind of triangle with the ground, and they were all made to fall in the same direction. In this way the trees piled up, each one on its neighbor, and produced a thicket that the caribou could not penetrate or jump over. Where the thicket was not tight enough, the Indians would weave branches from other trees into the fence.

If there were not enough trees for a fence, poles would be stuck at an angle into the ground and birch bark tassels tied to their tops. Flapping about in the wind like paper kites, they frightened the caribou, which would not dare to pass between the poles. Now the caribou could get to the river only where gaps had been left in the fences. Some Indians would hide in the forest and make loud noises to drive the caribou toward the fence; others would wait on the water in their canoes and spear the caribou as they crossed the river. This was easier than spearing them on land, because the animals could not move quickly in the water. If any of the caribou reached the other side of the river, there were more fences to stop them from escaping and more Indians behind "gazes" — rocks, turf and bushes piled up as hiding places. Bow and arrow were used to shoot any caribou that was passing along the river bank looking for a way into the forest.

This method of trapping and killing caribou was very effective, but the caribou do not come to a river exactly at the same spot where they crossed the previous year. To be prepared for the caribou at any point along the river, the Indians built the fences several miles long. On the river Exploits, which became the main hunting area of the Beothuck people, the fence works stretched along the banks for 30 miles. It must have taken a lot of people to make these fences and keep them in repair. Many family groups had to co-operate at each section; therefore the big fall hunt of caribou was a

Spearing caribou

16

Hunting seals on the ice

community affair. The Indians worked and hunted together and afterward shared the meat. They stayed together for the winter and built their winter wigwams close to each other, like houses in a village.

In spring the large camps were deserted while the Indians moved in smaller family groups to the coast to hunt harp seals. Today the sealing is mostly done from ships that travel north to search out the seal herds on the arctic ice fields, but the Beothucks hunted the seals that came on ice floes into the Newfoundland bays and close to shore. They pursued them in the water with their canoes and harpooned them from close range, or clubbed them on the ice floes.

A little later in the year, whales came into the coastal waters. They were highly prized by the Indians; depending on its size a single animal could feed a family for weeks. We know little about the methods that the Beothucks used in their whale hunt, but pods of the small whale species were probably driven into the shallows of a bay where they could be attacked with clubs and axes. Even today such groups of whales occasionally get stranded in shallow waters.

All through the summer sea birds such as murres, puffins, and sea pigeons were hunted with bow and arrow. The Indians would shoot them from a hiding place near the rock cliffs on which the birds liked to perch.

In early fall the wigwams along the shores were left behind as all the families returned to the inland rivers to meet for the caribou hunt. As well, the Beothuck Indians hunted other animals such as beaver, martin, fox and otter that were valued for their meat as well as their fur. The powerful black bear was also game for the Beothuck hunter. It must have taken courage for a hunter armed only with bow and arrow to attack a grown bear.

Throughout the winter various birds could be caught, especially a kind of grouse called the ptarmigan which lived in the forest. In Newfoundland's severe cold these birds lost much of their agility and could easily be knocked off the lower branches of the trees where they roosted.

Bird hunting

Arms and Tools

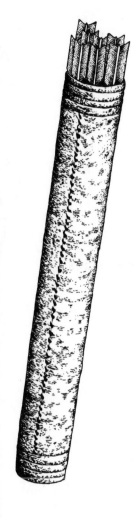

Quiver with arrows

Although different in many ways from the Indians of central Canada, the Beothuck people hunted and fought like others—with bows, arrows and spears. They were excellent archers who could aim and fire their arrows quickly. They held a few arrows in their left hand (the hand which also held the bow) and then passed one arrow after the other to the right hand, which set the notched and feathered end on the string, pulled it back and shot the arrow off. Their bows were made of a smoothed, seasoned spruce or mountain ash branch about 5½ feet long and tapered at each end. The bows were frequently rubbed with a grease and ochre mixture to prevent them from drying out. For bowstrings the Indians used animal sinews that they twisted and rolled together so that they would be strong and not stretch too much.

A large supply of arrows was carried in a quiver—a tube open at one end. The arrows were fashioned from well-seasoned pine and were slender, light and perfectly straight. One end was notched and had two strips of feather tied to it to give it balance. When an object was missed and an arrow fell into the water, the feathers kept it afloat in spite of the heavy stone or iron point. The hunter could then retrieve the arrow at his leisure.

Stone knife blade

Stone arrow head

19

Blunt arrow point

Stone arrow point

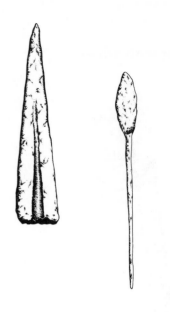

Originally the arrow points were made of stone or bone, but after the white settlers came, the Indians obtained iron from them to use as points for their weapons. They heated pieces of iron in the fire and beat them on a flat rock into pointed shapes. For hunting small birds, the Beothucks used arrows ending with a knob which would kill the bird without piercing it. Bows and arrows were the most frequently used hunting and fighting arms of the Beothuck Indians, because they could be shot from a fair distance or from an ambush.

The Beothuck Indians also had spears that were up to twelve feet long and fitted with large stone, bone or iron points. They were mainly used for hunting caribou from canoes. After paddling as close as possible, the hunter would thrust the spear into the animal with great strength, being careful not to tip the canoe.

When the Indians hunted seals they had to prevent the wounded seal from plunging down into the water to escape. They constructed special seal-hunting harpoons which they probably learned about from the Eskimos, who were experts in the seal hunt. The sharp harpoon head was made so that it detached easily from the wooden shaft, but it was tied to a long string of caribou skin which the hunter held firmly. The wooden harpoon shaft was used to thrust the sharp point into the seal, and the shaft

Iron arrow heads

Spear

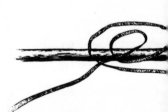

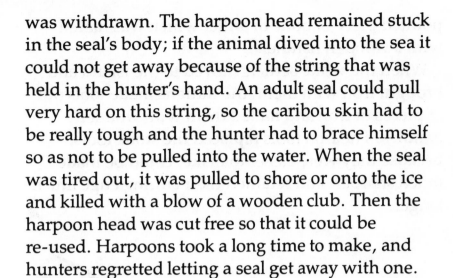

Iron arrow point

was withdrawn. The harpoon head remained stuck in the seal's body; if the animal dived into the sea it could not get away because of the string that was held in the hunter's hand. An adult seal could pull very hard on this string, so the caribou skin had to be really tough and the hunter had to brace himself so as not to be pulled into the water. When the seal was tired out, it was pulled to shore or onto the ice and killed with a blow of a wooden club. Then the harpoon head was cut free so that it could be re-used. Harpoons took a long time to make, and hunters regretted letting a seal get away with one.

For building canoes and wigwams, the Indians used hammering tools made with beach rocks of the best size and shape. Large cutting tools and small stone knives were made of flint or hard rock and were used to cut wood, bark, meat and skins. Sharp bones or stones served to scrape and prepare skins for clothing. To do small pieces of woodwork, the Indians chiseled with a beaver tooth. Strong enough to cut down trees, beaver teeth are very sharp and do not wear down easily. It is most likely that the Beothuck Indians used them to make "crooked" knives such as the versatile knives used by other woodland Indians. These knifes have a beaver tooth fitted on a wooden handle that is tapered and curved at the end. For cutting or shaving off wood, the blade is pulled sideways toward the user.

It seems that the Beothucks were not familiar with the bow drill that other Indians used to drill holes by rotating a pointed stick on an object. If they wanted to make a hole in a piece of bone, they used a knife to gouge out the hole; for material such as leather or bark they used an awl. An awl was made of a

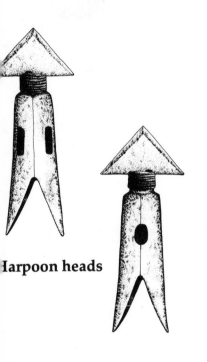

Harpoon heads

Harpoon

21

pointed piece of bone or antler which was hafted with a wooden handle.

When the white settlers moved to the island and brought iron with them, the Indians made tools out of pieces of iron and hafted them with wooden handles. The iron tools replaced the stone tools, because they were easier to make, could be made much sharper, and retained their cutting edge much longer.

Hafted stone knife

Crooked knife

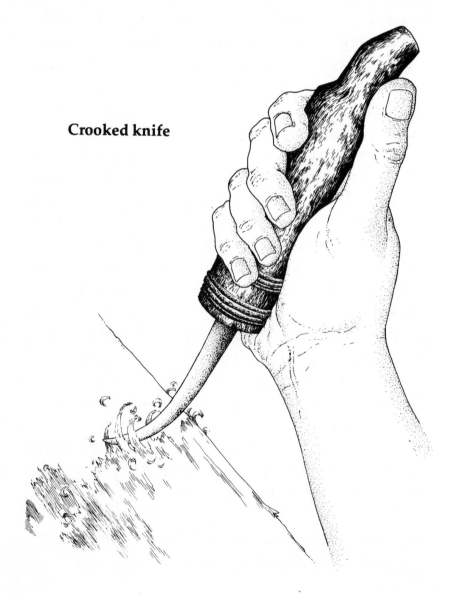

Housing

The Beothuck house was called a *mamateek*. The summer houses looked very much like the wigwams of other Indian tribes. Tall poles were stuck into the ground in a circle about 30 to 40 feet around, and were tied together at the top. Then sheets of birch bark were placed in layers like tiles over the structure. The top was left open so that smoke from the cooking fire could escape. The bark was held in position by more poles that were leaned against the outside of the mamateek. If no birch bark was available, the Indians used animal skins instead.

The fireplace was in the center of the mamateek and the sleeping places were formed by oblong hollows in the ground around it. To make the hollows more comfortable, the Indians lined them with the tender branches of fir or pine. There was room for six to ten people in such a mamateek. About one to three families camped together, each constructing its own mamateek. During the summer season the families moved about and probably had to build a new mamateek several times. A summer one could be completed in less than an hour and yet it was durable and warm.

The winter houses had to be sturdier and better insulated against heavy snowfalls and storms. They were also larger than summer habitations, as several families lived together in one mamateek. Built inland near a river or pond, they were many-sided, with six or sometimes eight sides, and measured about 22 feet across. Europeans who saw winter houses were surprised and impressed both by their size and by the sturdiness of their construction. Although the roofs were conical, like wigwams, the walls rose vertically. They were made of tree trunks driven upright into the ground close to each other.

The sides of the trunks were flattened to fit together well like those of a log cabin. The cone-shaped roof was made of a framework of poles which met in the center at the top. Hoops were used to hold the roofpoles together. The whole mamateek was covered with a triple coat of birch bark, with layers of moss and sods 6 inches thick placed between each coat. The smoke hole at the top was secured with clay.

In order to insulate the mamateek on the ground level, a bank of earth was thrown against the outside walls and all the cracks were stuffed with moss. With their inside walls covered with moss or caribou skins, the mamateeks were comfortable and warm. The Indians hung their bows and arrows, spears and tools on the walls. For the storage of food they made shelves by fitting beams crosswise inside the roof. The winter mamateek had a fireplace in the center with sleeping hollows around it, like the summer house. Each of the winter mamateeks was big enough for ten to twenty people, and up to ten of these houses were built close to each other.

Summer mamateek

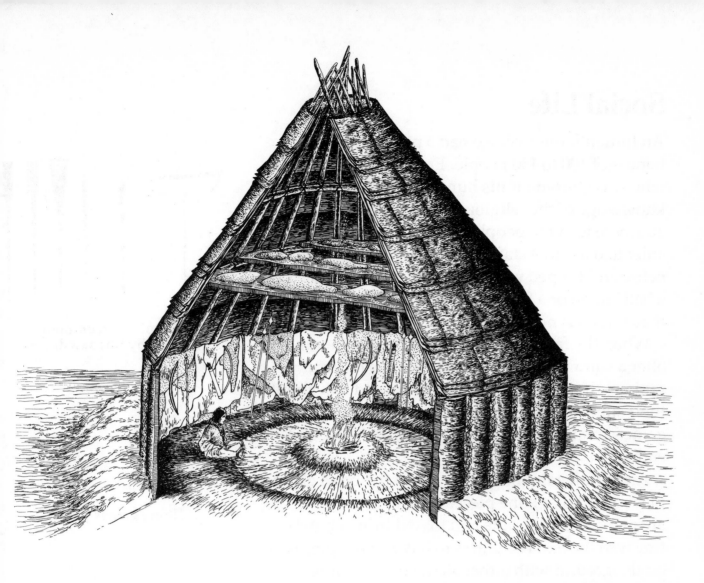

Winter mamateek, interior view

Social Life

An Indian winter village had a population—a band—of 100 to 150 people. Each band had a chief who was chosen for his hunting skills, his knowledge of the religious ceremonies, and his ability to lead the people in times of emergency. The chief had a 6-foot staff or emblem covered with red ochre and topped with a figure such as a whale's tail, a half-moon or a fishing boat. The exact meaning of these signs is not known to us.

When the families of a band came together in fall after a summer of living on the shores in small groups, they would exchange news and talk about their summer adventures. This was also the time for games and festivities with singing, dancing and eating.

An Indian gambling game called the bowl game is played with flat bone pieces or antler sections that are marked on one side and tossed from a bowl or tray into the air. The aim is to have all the pieces fall on the ground with either all the marked sides up or all the marked sides concealed. Each player receives points according to which way the games pieces fall. The Beothuck Indians carved small ivory blocks, patterned on one side, which were probably used for such a game.

Mythological emblems drawn by Shanawdithit

Bone games pieces

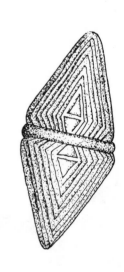

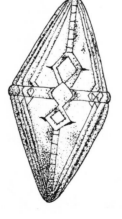

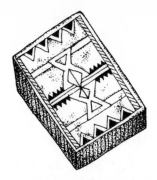

Games pieces

Songs were important for communicating and preserving beliefs and experiences. The Indians had songs about the animals which they hunted, about their tools and boats, and about mountains and water and all the things that were important in their daily lives. There were other songs, too, that told of famous deeds, of other tribes, and of the white man. In these songs the Indians remembered with pride the courage and cunning of their people. Sometimes a small group would sing its story, and at other times everybody would join in the song.

If an enemy had been killed, the Beothucks cut off his head as a trophy. When it was brought back to camp and stuck on a pole, they danced and sang around it to celebrate their victory.

Celebrating a victory

There were other occasions for feasting together. At a marriage everybody would join in the eating and merriment for a whole day and a night. Among the Beothucks, each man took only one wife. The women were respected as important partners in the family. They looked after the fire and prepared the food while the men went out hunting, and they made the clothes that were needed in wintertime. They cared for the young members of the family and were known for their love of children.

The old people remained part of the family. They helped with food preparation or made tools and weapons, and they would also give advice when a person was sick. The Indians knew of many plants and roots that helped to cure an illness or soothe a pain. They also used a steam bath for the treatment of aches and pains. Large rocks were piled up and a fire lit around them, to make the rocks very hot. Then the ashes were removed and a kind of tent of branches covered with skins was placed over the rocks. The patient would creep under the skins with a birch bark bucket of water and a small bark dish with which to dip the water onto the stones. Splashed with water, the hot rocks made steam. The density of the steam could be regulated by pouring more or less water onto the rocks.

Food

The Indians lived from hunting and gathering, so they ate mostly the foods of the season. In spring, fresh seal meat was a welcome change in the diet after a long winter with dried food and preserved caribou meat. Seals have a great deal of fat which the Indians rendered into oil and stored in bags made of seal bladders. The oil was used for food. It was also mixed with ochre, then rubbed onto body and clothes and all tools and implements. A whale would also supply large quantities of oil and fresh meat.

The sea offered a great variety of other foods as well, such as lobsters, clams, mussels and fish. Caplin—a kind of smelt—arrived every year in June in the bays and inlets to spawn along the water's edge. They came in such closely packed shoals that a person wading along the beach could pick them up with his hands. These small fish were followed by the cod who fed on them and could be fished all through the summer.

A favorite food for the Indians was the Atlantic salmon. Salmon come up the rivers to lay their eggs in shallow waters and are usually caught on their way up, in the mouths of rivers. Salmon not only provide a rich and delicious meal but also are well suited for preservation. Dried or smoked, they can be stored for the winter.

Thousands of sea birds inhabit Newfoundland's shores. They were much appreciated by the Indians for their meat as well as their eggs. These birds nest in large colonies on rock faces and cliffs. The Beothucks would seek out their nesting grounds and collect eggs in great numbers. The eggs were either eaten fresh or used in other ways. Sometimes they were combined with seal's fat, liver, fish and other ingredients and stuffed into seal intestines to make a kind of sausage. These sausages could be kept for times when fresh food was scarce. Eggs would also be boiled, mixed with caribou and seal fat, and then dried in the sun in the shape of small cakes. These cakes were their closest food to the white man's bread, for the Beothucks had no grain to make flour for baking. Egg yolks were boiled and crushed into powder to preserve them for later use; in this way the Indians produced a food reserve that was nourishing and easy to carry.

Wild berries are ripe in August and September in Newfoundland, and the Beothucks enjoyed blueberries, partridgeberries, marsh berries, raspberries, cranberries, wild currants, bake apples (cloud berries) and others. The Indians probably dried some of the berries to keep them for the winter and may have stored some in oil, because they had no sugar to preserve the berries. The Beothucks also collected roots from wild plants, and ate the inner bark of birch and spruce trees.

Beaver

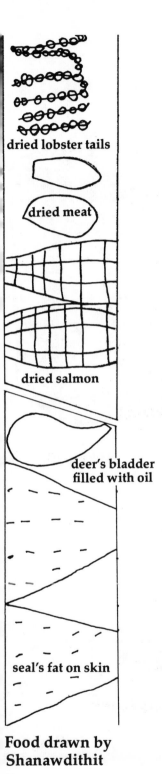

dried lobster tails

dried meat

dried salmon

deer's bladder
filled with oil

seal's fat on skin

**Food drawn by
Shanawdithit**

At this time of the year the Indians would move back into the forest to prepare for the winter. They hunted beaver and many smaller mammals; beaver meat was considered a delicacy.

Geese and ducks would flock together on the ponds on their way south and provide the Indians with plenty of fowl.

Once the herds of caribou returned from the barrens and neared the fence traps, the big hunt was on and the Indians were kept busy for weeks cutting and preserving the meat and skins. During the winter months they lived largely on caribou meat from the fall hunt. Some of the meat had to last until the following spring.

For cooking food, the Indians used an open fire. To start a fire they struck two pieces of iron pyrite together and caught the sparks with jay down or dry moss. When a good fire was going, they roasted large joints of meat over it on a wooden spit. The larger bones were cracked open because the Indians liked to eat the marrow. Smaller pieces of meat were pushed onto roasting sticks and placed around the fire to broil. The Indians also made soups from lean meat and bones. They heated stones in the fire and placed them in a birch bark pot to bring water and food to the boiling point. More hot rocks were added to keep the pot on the boil until the meat was done.

Birch bark was one of the Beothucks' most important raw materials, not only for making canoes and covering wigwams but also to wrap meat and to make household utensils. The bark was loosened from the living trunk with great care so as not to kill the tree, then cut into the desired shapes. One type of cup was folded from a rectangular piece of bark and then finely sewn with quartered rootlets. Other containers had a small tongue-like overlap of bark to cover the seams and make the vessel watertight. To make the bark dishes look attractive the Beothucks stitched decorations on them and cut the edges with a saw tooth pattern. Some vessels were small and used as cups; others were up to two feet high and served as water buckets or cooking pots.

Birch bark vesse

Boiling foo

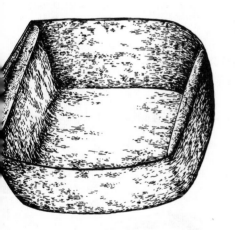

The Indians had several methods of keeping their meat from spoiling. Sometimes it was cut into thin strips, washed and then packed tightly with layers of melted fat into birch bark. Larger pieces of meat were taken from the bone and tied together in packages of up to two hundred pounds wrapped up in birch or spruce bark. As soon as the cold weather set in, these packages were exposed to the air. Once the meat was frozen, it would keep all winter.

Another method of preservation was to dry or smoke meat and fish in smoke houses. These houses were constructed of poles and had open latticework shelves which let air and smoke circulate freely. Fish or meat treated in this way would keep to the next season.

Foods and skins not only had to be preserved but also had to be stored so that animals could not get them. For this purpose, the Beothucks built storehouses of wood, usually close to where the caribou had been killed, and covered them with birch bark or animal skins. Some of these stores were as large as 40 or 50 feet square. Food was also kept next to the wigwams in oblong pits that were lined and covered with birch bark.

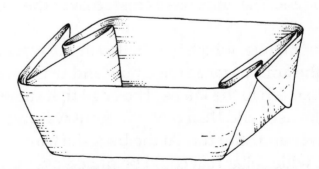

The folding of a birch bark vessel

Clothing

Winters in Newfoundland are cold, so the clothing of the Indians had to be very warm and protective. The Indians' main clothing material was caribou hide. The winter fur of the caribou is thick and light, and to make the best use of its warming quality, the Indians wore the fur part against their body. The leather outside was covered with a mixture of grease and ochre to keep it supple and to make it waterproof.

Preparing the skins and making clothes was usually the responsibility of the women. A fresh skin was scraped to get rid of all flesh and fat clinging to it. Then it was cured by rubbing the flesh side with animal brain or other tanning agents. It was stretched for drying on a wooden frame and the skin was then made soft and pliable by rubbing the leather side of the skin forcefully with a stone or bone tool. Chewing softened those parts which had to be especially pliable for sewing. When the skins were dry and soft, they were sewn together. Holes were pierced into the hide with an awl, and then a length of sinew was threaded through. It was a laborious job, so the Beothucks avoided extra seams. They just sewed two caribou hides together, and this formed a kind of mantle that was thrown over the shoulders. The ends were crossed over the chest, shawl-like.

The skin mantle, which was belted at the waist, covered the arms as far as the elbow and was long enough to reach to the knees. The edge that came around the neck and then down in front was trimmed with beaver and otter fur. At the back the trim formed a wide collar that could be pulled over the head in severe weather. The bottom edges of the coat were sometimes fringed by cuts made into the skins.

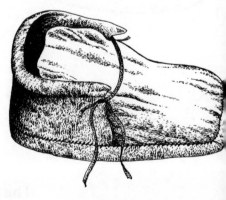

Child's moccasin

Hunter dressed in mantle of caribou hide

The Beothucks made winter leggings and arm coverings of caribou skins. They wore moccasins and mittens as well. In spring and summer they went naked except for a small skin suspended from a belt in front.

Chief in fur mantle and leggings, holding staff

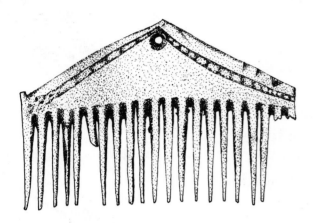

Combs

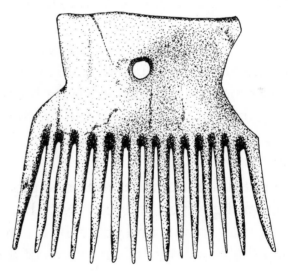

For combing their hair the Beothucks carved combs from pieces of bone or antler; these were sometimes decorated along the edge.

Arts and Beliefs

Bone carving was a skill that the Beothucks used in making harpoon heads and spear and arrow points. Small carved and decorated pendants were also made of bone and were exquisitely carved with very primitive tools; the surfaces were polished, and because all scratched or carved patterns were filled with red ochre, the design showed up well on the light, shiny bone. Most of the designs combine small geometrical patterns such as triangles, diamond shapes, ladders or zig zag lines. Among the hundreds of pendants that have been found, each single piece looks different from all others. A hole carved through at one end allows a thong to be attached. Nearly all pendants that are now in museum collections were found in graves, arranged as a necklace or tied to fringes or wrapped up in packages of about 30 and placed next to the deceased.

Because we have no certain knowledge about the religious beliefs of the Beothuck Indians, we compare their practices and artifacts with those of other tribes. If their life style, habits and artifacts were similar, we assume that their beliefs may have been similar too.

We therefore think that the carved bone pieces had a symbolic meaning which had to do with Beothuck beliefs that animals, plants and other things in nature all had their own spirits, and some of these were more powerful than others. Shapes and patterns for these bone pieces were handed down from one generation to the next. We are not able to interpret the patterns because no Beothuck Indian disclosed their meaning to a white person, but some of the pendants look very much like the claws of a bear. The bear was considered to be important in the

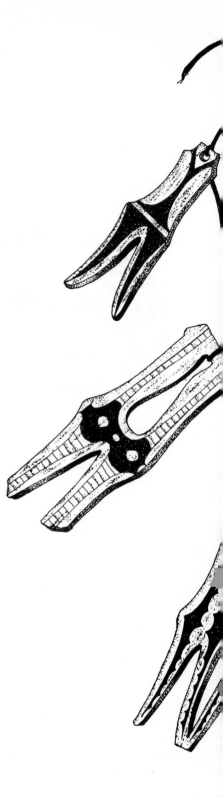

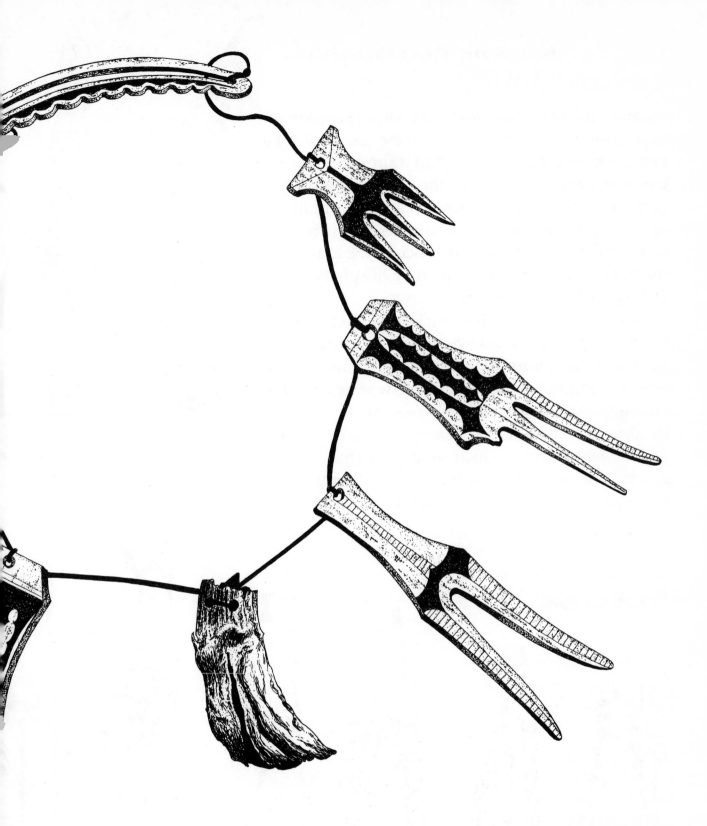

Bone pendant necklace

Bone pendants shaped like bear claws

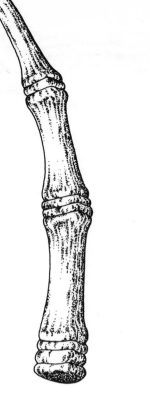

animal world and most northern native people used to perform bear ceremonies to please his spirit. The Beothuck people most likely had a similar respect for the bear and may have used the claw-shaped carvings as bear symbols. Other carvings might be simplified figures of various animals or spirits. They were probably used as good-luck charms to help in the hunt, or as amulets to fend off evil spirits, or to give special powers to their wearers.

We do know that the Beothucks assumed that a Great Spirit held control over much of nature and man. They also feared a kind of Red Indian "devil" who would punish the wicked. He was described as wearing a black cloak and a long beard. The Beothucks had a story of their origin—they spoke of a cluster of arrows which were stuck into the ground and which turned into people. In myth, these people were their very early forefathers.

Bone pendants

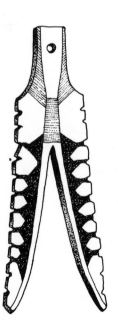
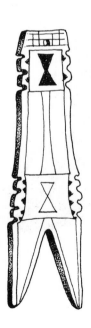
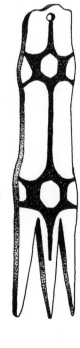

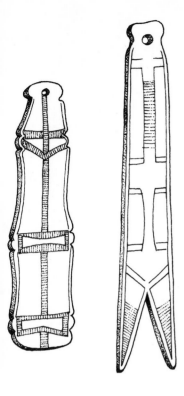

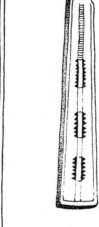

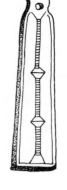

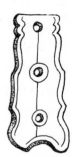

Bone pendants

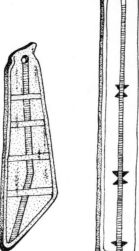

For the Beothuck people, death was only a form of sleep and they expected life to continue in some way. They buried their dead with great care. The body of the deceased was covered with red ochre, wrapped in birch bark or skin, and covered with large rocks in a shallow grave. Food, everyday articles, weapons, beads and bone amulets were included in the graves for later use and for spiritual protection. Graves of the Beothucks have been found along the coast in caves and rock shelters, and it is thought that the Indians often brought their dead in the spring season to the shore to bury them near the sea.

The Beothucks had different ways of placing the body in a grave which probably depended upon whether the person had been an important member of the tribe and whether it had been a hunter or woman or child.

The grave of a young boy was found on a small island with his well-preserved body lying on its side inside an ochre-stained beaver skin bag. The bag had fringes and there were bone amulets and birds'

Carved wooden figure placed in child's grave

feet tied to it. The burial place contained small bows and arrows, packages of food and ochre, canoe models and paddles, bark cups and a carved wooden figure. On another island an adult Indian was found in a sitting position in the ground with a grass rope under him and going up over his head. All bones were rubbed with red ochre and the skeleton was covered with a caribou skin. A broken bow and some arrows had been placed at his side, and there were bone pendants and small, flat beads made from shell, bone, and wood shoots. The beads were strung like a necklace with a clam shell disk at each end, and they were heavily stained with ochre. These bead strings are very much like the wampum strings that were used by other tribes as ornaments or in ceremonies.

Cross-section of Beothuck burial

Although most of the graves have been found near the sea, inland cemeteries discovered in the early 1800s contained bodies in burial huts or lying on platforms several feet off the ground. Ochre was always part of the grave goods, and the bones of the deceased were stained with ochre.

String of beads or wampum

Contacts with White People

The Vikings were the first white people to discover Newfoundland. We do not know whether they ever met with the Beothuck Indians when they visited the island around 1000 AD. Much later, in 1497, John Cabot came upon the coast of Newfoundland and brought back to England the news of unexplored northern lands. His report inspired many others to follow him. Soon it was known that the Terra Nova or New Land had much useful timber and large fishing grounds. Within a century, extensive fishing fleets from England, Portugal, France and Spain fished the Newfoundland waters every summer. Several of the ships captured natives to bring them back to Europe as slaves, or to exhibit them as curiosities.

The first recorded settlement on the island was founded in 1610 by John Guy, who met with the Beothucks and started a trade. He wanted their animal furs, and the Indians received in exchange knives, axes, needles, scissors, and clothes. He arranged through signs that they should meet again the following year. The Beothucks came back to the trading place at the appointed time, but by chance another fishing ship arrived. Seeing so many Indians assembled and believing them to be hostile, the captain had the ship's cannon fired into the crowd. The Indians fled, and peaceful trade with the Beothuck people was ruined.

In the 1700s many farmers, fishermen and trappers made Newfoundland their new home. They built communities in the sheltered bays and inlets which had been the summer residences of the Beothucks, forcing the Indians to move into more remote parts of the island. As more settlers followed and populated most of the coastal areas, the Beothucks could not live along the seashores as they used to. This meant that they were not able to collect enough food during the summer season to feed themselves and have a surplus for the winter. The Indians began to starve. When diseases such as tuberculosis were brought to the island by the white people, many Beothuck Indians died.

Many of the settlers were afraid of the Red Indians. They would have liked to take over their hunting grounds and they also felt angry whenever a Beothuck stole a tool or other useful items. This caused some of the white people to hunt down the Indians and to kill them and destroy their wigwams and canoes whenever they came upon them. Many reports tell of cruel deeds committed against Indian men, women and children.

While Indians of other tribes adapted themselves to the white newcomers and traded and intermingled with them, the Beothucks shied away from the white people. Their terrible experiences made them retreat and keep up their traditional way of life as best as they could. They defended themselves when they met with the settlers, and sometimes killed in revenge. The Micmac Indians who moved up from the southwest coast into Beothuck territory became enemies of the Beothuck and were another threat to them.

Although the Beothuck Indians were skilled with their bows and arrows, they could not hold out against enemies with guns, and their tribe was rapidly reduced in numbers. The government became concerned and tried to protect the Beothucks by ordering all white people and other Indian tribes not to harm or kill any of them. But the government was too far away to enforce the order, and the

persecutions continued.

During earlier centuries there may have been up to a thousand Beothuck people on the island of Newfoundland. By the time the colonial government started to take an interest in these Indians, there were only a few hundred of them left. In 1768, Capt. John Cartwright from the British navy was sent into the interior to find their camps and befriend the Indians, but his mission failed because he did not meet with any of them.

In the winter of 1810, Capt. David Buchan with a company of Marines made contact with some of the Indians inland. He tried to convince them of his good intentions, but the Beothucks were much too frightened to believe him. They killed two of his men and fled.

The last person to attempt to meet with the Beothucks was William Epps Cormack, a Scot whose heart went out to the native people and who founded the "Beothuck Institution" to help them. In 1827, he searched the forests and valleys for an Indian camp, climbing the hills to try to spot telltale smoke. His exhausting expedition was in vain. The Red Indians could no longer be found.

Much of what we know about the Beothucks was learned from reports of early settlers and by those who went inland in search of the Indians. They described how the Beothucks lived, what their houses, canoes, clothes and arms looked like, and what animals they hunted and ate.

Other information was given by two unfortunate Beothuck women who were captured in the early 1800s and who lived for a while in white communities.

Demasduit was taken prisoner in March 1819 by a

Summer mamateek, inside view

group of fishermen and trappers who were in pursuit of the Indians. They called her "Mary March" because she was captured in the month of March. Her husband, Nonos-a-ba-sut, who was a chief, was killed when he came to Demasduit's aid, and her baby was left behind and died shortly afterward. Demasduit was tall and had delicate limbs and a musical voice. She was gentle and intelligent, and easily learned the English words that she was taught. A long list of Beothuck words and their meanings was collected from her and this has helped to relate the Beothuck language to that of other Algonquin tribes. A portrait of Demasduit was made during her brief visit to St. John's; it is the only authentic picture of a Beothuck Indian in existence.

Portrait of Demasduit

It had been the intention of the Newfoundland people to make friends with Demasduit and then return her to her tribe so that she could report about the friendliness and good will of her captors. But before Demasduit could rejoin her people she died of tuberculosis and a party was dispatched to carry her coffin back into Indian country.

In 1823, three starving Beothuck women were taken captive. One of these, a girl of about 20 years, survived. Her name was Shanawdithit and she lived for five years with a settler's family who called her Nancy. Shanawdithit was a lively person,

**Dancing woman,
drawn by Shanawdithit**

**Red Indian "devil"
drawn by Shanawdithit**

industrious and intelligent. She loved children and was described as gentle and having a natural gift for drawing. She was afraid to return to her tribe because she feared that she would not be forgiven for having lived with white people. Sometimes she was overcome with melancholy and would slip into the woods to converse with her dead mother and sister.

When W.E. Cormack came back from his trip inland in 1827, people realized that Shanawdithit might be one of the last of the Beothuck Indians. She was brought to St. John's and looked after by Cormack, to whom she told much of what she knew about the Beothuck tribe. Shanawdithit made a series of drawings which depicted earlier encounters between the Indians and the white people. Other drawings showed mamateeks, food, utensils and chiefs' emblems. She also drew a picture of the Red Indian "devil" and a dancing woman, but her explanations of the pictures cannot be fully understood. Cormack wrote down many of the things she said, including part of the Beothuck language. Some of his notes were later published, but others have disappeared. The lost notes contain irreplaceable knowledge about the Beothuck people. Since these notes may still be in existence in an attic or an archive, many people have tried to trace them, but without success.

In St. John's, Shanawdithit fell ill with tuberculosis, and died in 1829. No more Beothuck Indians were met with after this date. It is possible that a few survivors managed to leave Newfoundland and join other Indians in Labrador, but the Beothuck Indians as an independent tribe had vanished forever.

Acknowledgments

Drawings of Beothuck Indian artifacts were made
from eighteenth and nineteenth century documents
and from collections with the permission of:
Museum of Mankind, British Museum, London,
England
National Museum of Man, Ottawa, Ontario
Newfoundland Museum, St. John's, Newfoundland
Public Archives Canada, Ottawa, Ontario
Dr. J. Templeton, Winnipeg, Alberta

Shanawdithit's drawings were copied from J.P.
Howley's *The Beothucks or Red Indians*, Cambridge,
1915.